Sassy Sally
Glad to have met you

Mark Hayn

1

Introduction Welcome Poem

Sometimes you will find it's good to simply
unwind, kick back in an easy chair;
in pajamas with no stress, thoughts or cares.
The dishes can wait and the laundry too this is a
time to focus on you.
Coffee, tea maybe a little dinner wine
to settle down and clear your mind.
Now the mood is set and the time is right;
pick up my book of
"*Soulful and Sassy Reflections and Poems*"
and read to your heart's delight.
These stories and poems came to you from
God above; an expression of his
goodness, grace and His love.
~

This is a poetry book that includes poems and a
few short stories of cultural clarity and
understanding all for the purpose of
encouraging faith and inspiration to strengthen
anyone that needs an emotional, spiritual lift.

Gail Haynes – Author

ISBN: 9781730926693

AMAZON ~ KINDLE PUBLISHING

Acknowledgements:

I want thank Dee Williams who assisted me with countless hours of direction, guidance and wisdom.

I want to thank Byron Botler who spent many hours editing and educating. I want to thank Mauris Emeka for his continual support and encouragement.

Special thanks to all my family and friends who have inspired me. There are too many to name but you know who you are.

I want to thank the members of the African American Writer's Alliance (AAWA) who have inspired me to write and expand to authorship. This is where my roots of public writing and speaking began. This organization helped me to further recognize my love of the art of writing and spoken word.

Most of all I want to give thanks, honor and glory to God and my Lord Jesus Christ for giving me the gift of poetry.

Table of Contents

Little Flower
When you need God's deliverance

I was once a little flower crushed, trampled on the ground; I lived in sadness my face in a frown; I cried to God He said, "No More" your life my child, I will restore. He awakened me and called me by name; He said my child your life will never be the same.

Today I'm free in Jesus name He opened the doors that I might live; He gave me a heart of love that I may give.

Thank you Jesus for dying on the cross; for saving my soul when I was lost. Jesus said I sent the warmth of my sunshine; I sent the refreshing of my rain; I sent the breeze of the wind to wipe away all your pain.

I'm the one who blocked the darkness when you couldn't see; I'm the one who defeated the devil and told him to flee. Open your petals accept my love; angels are smiling from heaven above Now I can smile, laugh, sing and dance.

He said go out and look around; seek other flowers crushed, trampled on the ground.

Share my sunshine and share my rain; Share my breeze that wiped away your pain; Tell them I love them just the same; Tell them they're free in Jesus Name.

6

Yesterday
Remembering those who have passed on

I was here yesterday but today I've gone away.
It was time for me to go home,

My body was weak, tired and worn.
It's been a long journey at times it's been rough.

Yesterday I ate my last meal and
drank from my last cup.
While you're in the land of the living;
Mend your ways and be about forgiving.

If I ever hurt you please forgive me;
I forgive you too, now we are both free.

Let love find itself in your hearts, for those around you
and the ones who have departed.

Remember you are here for a season and a time;
allow kindness, love and peace fill your mind.
For just like me the clock will stop for you, your time
will be up and your days will be through.

Good bye my loved ones I've gone home;
my address has changed,
I've disconnected my phone.

Remember my laugh, remember my smile
Remember the times we chatted awhile.

Just breathe
Stop, pause and take it in

You may have seasons of darkness,

sadness and despair.

Feelings of frustration to the point of

pulling out your hair.

You may have lost a loved one and times are rough.

But you'll only go so far and God will say that's enough.

Deeply breathe in and close your eyes

Exhale slowly and smile

God can give you peace in the midst of the storm.

His peace will keep you warm.

He's a Playa (Player)
When you should wake up and move on

Ladies, I need you to stop and hear me say don't easily
give your love away. You my sister are a jewel;
not a play thing or someone's fool.

Surrender yourselves to make a bold stand;
Wait for the Lord to send you a good man.
I want to share an experience from long ago
about a man I used to know.

This man will whisper sweet nothings in your ear;
stuff you know is a lie but sometimes you may want to
hear. He was a street hustler drawn to petty crime
always hustling and asking me for a dollar or a dime.

I said get a job he says *"Honey I don't have the time"*.

C'mon baby give me some money I got to make a run;
time is wasting; no time for fun.
I got to move fast and make this deal;
you know I'm a playa, let's keep it real.

There is a street reputation, baby that bears my name;
now don't get mad it's all in the game;
I'm so big I'm in the playa's hall of fame.

He said you don't understand, I'm playa #3 - 1st was
grandpa, big daddy then me; this life I inherited and
was passed down to me. The square life is not who I
am; I'm what you call a playa man.
My clothes are clean, my shoes are shined,
my hair is laid, "Baby you know I'm fine"

I graduated from street school, hard living has corrupted my mind. I'm highly street educated from the finest hustlers and the top of the line.

He was wasting time drifting day to day seeking the next con and who he can play. It's a sad thing he didn't know; so much potential he didn't show.

Standing in front of the liquor store,
hands in his pockets shaking change.
No focus for his future, no goals to be explained.
Just day-to-day hustling, gambling, drinking cheap wine; his clothes nice and clean, his shoes highly shined.

He was tall, dark handsome, well-built and all that. He would wink his eye, smile and tip his hat. I assessed my situation and I began to see; this is not the way my life was supposed to be. I'm open for a godly man whose kind and violence free; who respects all women and celebrates me.

I got some sense and said for sure;
I'll pack my bags and head for the door.
The dreams, the self-esteem, I lost I had to get back.
I must say yes, I got off track. His finesse, his looks and sometimes he was even kind.
But it's all in the game I must have lost my mind.
When I later talked to him he said "Baby, where did you go so fast" I had big plans, you were the star in my cast.

I said don't you worry it's all in the past.
I thank God Almighty I'm free at last.

Purpose
Walk in it with splendor and grace

God lifted my head but it came back down;
a smile on my face always landed in a frown. One day
sunshine came in and changed my life; gave me
footing, self-love, peace, without strife. My mind
opened up thru God's great light; I became
empowered, enlightened, with high hopes in sight.

To love is to allow myself to live and be free, to stretch
out my limbs and allow real love to increase in me.
It was time to redefine my life? To refuse any sort of
confusion, chaos and strife. I will not be captivated in a
cell made by human hands, shaped by human minds,
strapped down with iron bands. God has blessed and
created me to live a life of victory.
I'm not arrogant just glad to be me.
I'm calling all men and women yellow, red, black,
white and brown; hold on to your power and refuse to
lose your ground. The Queen/King in you wants to
come out; take a stand give a shout let em' know what
you're all about. You are a fine walking wonder, a
work in progress, shaking up thangs, making your own
thunder. You are significant, outstanding, stunning and
fine. It's time my brother and sister to let your light shine.
You are blessed and highly favored, custom-made by
God the Master Tailor.
Take up the dreams you once let go. Accentuate
yourself don't just go with the flow go with the
knowledge that you know. Use the potential you have
within believe that you were created to win.

11

Poems by my daughter, Shurvon Haynes

Spirit of God The Spirit of God within you is STRONG ENOUGH To provide all the nutrients, vitamins and minerals to feed your Mind, Body, Heart and Soul with strength, courage and wisdom.

~Fall Fiesta Queen~ "We are all one color many different shades. Sienna, Mahogany, Cinnamon and Gold. Brilliant, Bright Bodacious and Bold." The summer to love was a beautiful dream but now it's time for the reign of the Fall Fiesta Queen. "She has no reason to be sad, heartbroken and bitter, because she is a jewel that shines in a gold mine with a laugh like a southern belle and a soul that sparkles like glitter."

~Love~ Love is true; fragile and blue; shiny, clear, safe and new.

Sisterhood

Lady, woman, sister and friend to define a female where does one begin? Single, married, daughter or mother we can all relate to each other. Love, Live, laugh or sing learn from our differences we each bring. Young, old, thick and thin there is a place for us all to fit in A queen, virtuous courageous and bold; she is more precious than silver and gold. She presses forward no looking back; because she's confident and fears no lack. Her words are sweet; she dwells among the wise Knows who she is; no need for disguise. Males, men brothers are good; but it sure feels great to be a part of the sisterhood.

12

Shurvon Haynes

Daddy's Arms
There's no comfort aside from the Lord's

When the world around me is in alarm and enemies

threaten to do me harm.

I find safety when I crawl into my daddy's arms.

When strife and confusion bring sudden fear my Daddy

reaches out and draws me near wiping away all my
tears.

In his arms that's my secret place,

where I find strength to run this race.

My Daddy, Creator, Lord and King.

To him alone my praises sing.

There is no other place I'd rather be and no other face

I'd rather see, than my daddy's who is holding me

close and loving me when I need him most.

Shurvon Haynes

Pray for our children
They need us even though they think they're grown

Little children far and near; crying out for us to hear.
They need our strength, wisdom and love;
they came from heaven, Father God above.

Let's train them in the way they should go that God's
purpose for them will flow.

No sagging pants, drugs and wine; that's not God's will
for their minds.

Teen moms need our guidance; don't put them down,
teach don't preach; lead them on to solid ground.

Pray for all the children in the land; let's commit
them into God's hands.

Remember the days when you were a child, running
the streets acting wild.

Someone prayed that you would make it thru; crying
out for your soul, that God's love would make you
whole.

So when you see a child going astray take the time to
stop and pray for their protection, God's guidance and
direction, to know Him like you do; that one day they
will make it thru.

The Team

When you know you ate too much but it's too late

At the movies there was hot buttered cheesy popcorn,
Dinner was mashed potatoes and steak, dessert was
ice cream and cake, it was enough to give me a belly-
ache. Later on there was buttermilk biscuits, fried pork
chops and corn, the stomach; grumbled to the liver
I can't take it anymore. I'd love a lite salad and baked
fish; can't he have that kind of dish?

Ouch! says the stomach, does he think I'm made of
steel? I need a digestion pill. Then the pancreas chimes
in as if that wasn't enough I took down a huge piece of
apple pie it was so sweet I thought I would die,
I struggled to keep the blood sugar from climbing too
high

The liver says were a team
we can stand this test.
On I don't know says the heart as it
beat hard in the chest, I could use some rest.

Oh the stomach says, wait! It feels like a treadmill with
running feet; the organs breathed a sigh of relief;
for weeks there was salads, baked chicken; no pork or
beef.

There was fresh fruit, yogurt with granola and lots of
water throughout; the stomach says this is what I'm
talking about.

Yes, says the liver this is peace; I can know
relax and have a release
The pancreas says whew! I'm overworked as if working
for two. The heart became sound; and the blood
pressure went down.

They all accepted the change "Hallelujah"
they all sang. Weeks later the organs began to shake
oh no! says the stomach is this an earthquake?

Thunder hit the thighs; the stomach begins to swell;
the pancreas says I don't know what's happening I
cannot tell. The liver says this is no fun but I'm stuck I
can't run. The kidneys were quiet, they said don't worry
we got your back; remember we are a team maybe
it's a gall-bladder attack.

We must access the brain about this situation as
the colon cries *help* I have constipation.
The brain reports this is not the gall bladder attack or
the flu; what is happening is nothing new,
in no time all of you will make it thru.

I know what has disturbed your peaceful living;
It's simply called *"Thanksgiving"*

We were delicately designed by God above; who
designed each of us with his great love.
We are tough and strong we can stand the test
they paused, listened then calmed down to rest.

GOD'S PEACE

No one can give you peace like the Lord

It's here and there; the peace
of God is everywhere. It's with me when I'm awake,
His peace does not take a break.

His peace is with me when I'm depressed
to calm my nerves to escape from a mess.
This peace comes only from you
to encourage me when I'm feeling blue.

It covers me when I'm at home He assures me I'm
never alone. His peace is with me everywhere but not
only for me but with you I share. Cast all your cares;
your grief He bears. His yoke is easy; His burdens light.

When I need Him He can be found; you can sense His
love and presence all around. He has put a clapping
in my hands and a running in my feet.

He is the one who makes my heart beat. He holds you
up with all His might from the north, east, south and
west. Accept God's Peace to give you rest.

He will take your pain that is deep and calm your mind
so you can sleep. He holds you in the palm of His hand
so you can have the strength to stand. The world's
peace fades away but God's peace comes to stay.

The Glory of His Presence

Stand in the awe of His presence

Today is the day to stand up and shout,

That our Lord Jesus is the everlasting King!

Rise up and dance, clap your hands and sing,

Praise the Lord let the bells ring.

He shines in His glory with his angels around,

To stand in His presence you're on holy ground.

You are the redeemed of the Lord let the trumpet

sound, you are in the presence of the King

standing on Holy Ground.

The demons tremble at the sound of His name,

they run and hide as his Name is proclaimed.

Jesus the Lord our conqueror and King.

Stand up with boldness you have the victory.

A Wedding Poem

When you met Mr. Right

I am bone of your bone and flesh of your flesh;

When God gave me you He gave me His best.

What God has joined together no one can divide;

He is the center of our love in Him we will abide.

I'm captured by your love sweetheart take my hand;

I'm thankful and blessed you are my man.

I submit to you ever so sweetly;

Only through God can I love you completely.

I stand before God, witnesses and friends;

I am your wife, lover and friend until the end.

HE WATCHES

God is omnipresent; meaning He is everywhere present

The mother eagle is very wise;

her baby eagle she will guide.

The mother bear watches her young;

as they play and frolic in the sun.

I cannot see God but He watches me;

He can see around corners I cannot see.

The atheist says God's not real;

but I stand strong to make a bold appeal;

That the God I serve is sure enough real

From sun up till sundown

God is here and there;

His presence is everywhere.

"Let him go"
When you have reached your limit

Wait a minute, are you serious is this how love is
supposed to be fighting,
arguing putting your hands on me?

You're mad because one crumb is on the floor; the kids
are upset and scared they don't want to play no more.
This is a time I need to reflect on me
Through the tears I look in the mirror and what do I see.

I see a strong, capable woman looking back at me.
I'm busy getting my college education
I don't need your ego tripping, control and
aggravation.

I've been patient with all your mess, seriously it's
causing me lots of stress. You don't need violence to
validate your manhood. Try a sweet attitude and some
tenderness if you would.

I want to be respected, when you call my name.
I'm not looking for accolades, applause or fame. God
is my husband, the door opener for my life; I may be
your girlfriend but I'm sure not your wife.

I was born to live a life that's happy and free;
If you don't like it get your coat and flee.

Yes that's right...miss me baby the door is open for you,
keep on stepping because we are through.

The power in me

Psalms 139 verses 13,14 "You are Fearfully and Wonderfully made

Dear God, what is in me that reflects you?

Child you are the Called of the Lord the everlasting King.

I made you in your mother's womb, to be a light to

others to lift up and encourage your

sisters and brothers.

Hold up your head, chest up, stand tall, I'm the Lord

who will catch you when you fall.

Cast down your thoughts of sadness and despair,

Smile and know I love you and I'm always near.

I broke the yoke off your back so you can be free,

free to be who I created you to be.
You have a calling to set the captives free.

God's Sunshine

In God's sunlight you won't get sun burned

You are God's sunshine meant to shine bright; you may

feel down sometimes but hold on to His light.

Though times may be hard keep this fact in sight,

that you are God's sunshine a light that shines bright.

So rise up and see a better day, put away worries and

determine to stay in the sunshine of God's light,

to be a blessing to those who have lost sight.

Rise up smile and shine thru the clouds and rain;

Rise up and shine thru the tears and pain.

You are God's sunshine meant to shine bright he loves

you dearly hold on to His light.

A Woman of God
A woman of substance, value and grace

She's confident and sure; she stands on God's Word as
she blesses the poor.

She's extraordinary, a cut above the rest;
a Woman of God; highly favored and blessed. It's not
her outward appearance;
No! it's deeper than that; it's the beauty of her inner
spirit that makes people say, *Who is that?*

She's a woman of God most
confident and sure; she stands on God's Word
as she blesses the poor.
You won't see this woman in the night clubs
dropping it like it's hot.

A worldly woman she is not!
She's wise, discerning, loving and kind
in her heart is a place where
Almighty God resides.

She carries herself with reverence and respect;
not as a loose woman exposing her best.
Her children arise and honor her name;
they stand proud of this woman with no shame.

She goes in her secret place, falling on her knees;
crying out to God for her family and their needs. Praise
this woman of God from afar and near; for this is the
kind of woman God holds most dear.

God's Man

A man of character, strength and honor

His phone is ringing here he comes; shoulders squared back and stepping strong; an appointment with destiny, no time to waste; lives at stake and bondages to break.

There's no slump, no swag in his walk; no slang or idle, crazy talk, for he walks and talks with a purpose; he moves with a plan. Who is this man? He is God's man.

No slipping or sliding, ducking and hiding. God's man is faithful not into playing games, He honors his ministry, his woman and his children and brings glory to God's Name.

He's a man who moves in and under the authority of God; The Bible, a weapon of warfare he carries so proud. Who is this man who speaks so bold, walks so tough with a heart full of gold; Be not mistaken this is not a man of the world; who finds time to chase after women and girls.

This man is anointed, called and appointed, his commission comes from heaven above; he moves with compassion and heart-felt convictions as he reaches out to others in love.

He's known in the city and is respected in the land; the elders wait to welcome him and shake his hand. Who is this man? He is God's man, a man with a purpose, a man with a plan.

Jesus is all I need

You are the strength that keeps me strong;
you hold me up all the day long.
without you where would I be;
where would I go and who would I see.
You order my footsteps from one place to the next; to
do your will is always best.

One step at a time

He's with us every step of the way

Wake up my child it's a new day
open your eyes it's time to pray.
You may have layers of burdens, worries and cares, it's
like when you come upon many stairs. One step at a
time you can trust God to see you thru. There will be
many times you won't know what to do.
Take one step not two or three patience will bring a
breakthrough you will see.
Don't ask why you'll know by and by,
and remember my child it's ok to cry,
for crying helps to ease the pain;
so relax and allow God's presence to reign.

As you climb those stairs you will find that His yoke is
easy His burden is light; don't try to be strong and put
up a fight because He can put 10,000 demons to flight
with His power and might.

When you reached the top of the stairs and your trials
are done just know thru God the victory is won.

Safe in His Hands

No one can snatch you from God's hands
John 10:28-30 KJV Bible

Mighty and powerful is your name. You hold the world
in your hands. At the name of Jesus people will stand.
Demons will fall at your every command.
He's the Alpha and Omega
our beginning and our end. When the trumpet sounds
every knee will bend. He's the light who conquers
darkness, his reign will never end.

This is Jesus don't be mistaken he is the son of God. He
loves all people both here and abroad. I wake up and
think of His great love who snatched me from hell,
I'm a living witness to the world I will tell.

As far as I can understand God has kept me in His
hands. He's protected me as far I can remember from
January to December.

As we sit in the Maker's hands we are secure. The
power of his might makes us feel assured.

Seasons will change but God will be by our side. Some
people are fickle they will slip and slide. God will not
forsake us or leave us alone.

He says, *"Child I'm with you until you come home"*

Let the truth be told
It's a blessing to get old

Birthdays come and birthdays go; I'm looking forward to
another one; and I'm not done having my fun,
There may be a time to nurse our ills, take cod liver oil,
Rub on Ben-gay, take a few pills.
That's ok you can still dress and hold your head up high and
strut like vintage wine, all the way past ninety-nine.
I'll add a "G" to the word old and rename it Gold
For when you become old you've earned the privilege
of living in your golden years.
It's also like seasoned Louisiana red beans and rice with
sweet corn bread on the side for when you've become old
you've obtained a special kind of flavor,
a flavor that only the seasoned ones can savor.
Age is only a number and an attitude of the mind.
And to make it real; it is how you feel
For let the truth be told; it's a blessing to get old.
I want my Social Security benefits and Medicare I struggled
and worked hard to get there.
I have much to do and people to see God has saved my
life and made me free. If you want to wear your hair short,
long or in between or color it black, red or maybe even
green; your hair can be weaved and whipped with
highlights of gold or wear it gray don't explain it's your right
you can wear it that way. You're free to be who you want
to be. *All I want is the truth to be told; it is a blessing to get
old.* I told my grandson at age two; grandma is ok but I'm
Nana to you. Age is a number and an attitude of the mind,
get up shake yourself and unwind. Stand up and be
counted, bust a move; rise up and fly; you have much to do
before your final good bye. Make life count and come
alive, move with grace as the years go by and while you're
at it keep strutting your stuff while the truth be told
remember you're gold and seasoned and it's a blessing to
be getting old

He's my brother; he's unique like no other
"Mom's pride and joy"

Keith and I and three siblings were born and raised in
the Yesler Terrace housing projects many years ago, a
place people viewed as a bad neighborhood but if
they didn't live there what do they really know;
We believed we were rich even though we were poor.
It's like Jesus being born in a manger with cows and
chickens at his bedside. He came to be the Messiah,
God the Father and Holy Spirit as our guide, to make it
plain He's always by our side. We were five kids with
mom in a two bedroom apartment living among family
and friends, a time back in the sixties when people
looked out for neighbor's kids. Keith is the fourth child,
third boy, undoubtedly, mom's pride and joy.
He was selfish didn't want no one to touch his stuff but
my sister, Linda and I called his bluff.
His comic books were all his own,
He wasn't open to giving us a small loan.
Keith is a smart man with a plan, an entrepreneur who
can make a fortune selling anything that's not nailed
down. When it comes to selling seriously he should
have a crown. This is his skill, when he comes to a yard
sale he's ready for the kill. He has a gift to draw people
to buy his used treasures. They go home happy,
grinning with lots of pleasures. He has many talents and
gifts rolled into one plus a sense of humor which makes
him a lot of fun. If you need anything fixed Keith is the
man, he has a natural skill that can shame a
professional man's plan. He's a good catch for a
special lady, he's gentle, sweet and he's keen, meet
him for a date at a yard sale and he will make you his
queen.

Children need to know the truth
Cultural awakening

As a child I wondered why my mom encouraged me often to pinch my nose. She said squeezing it will make it straight like white folks. Puzzled, I had to breathe out my mouth for a few seconds every day as I looked in the mirror squeezing my nose. I looked at her nose which was significantly wider than mine. I didn't ask if she pinched her nose because I figured if she did she would share her progress.

I wondered why it was important for my nose shape to change. The thought never came to me that God made a mistake in creating me. I later learned this was judged by some people as a negative facial feature...why? My thought was since I'm able to smell anything it should be ok. What in heaven's name is a nose for anyway? to me it was alright.
Then I learned my hair was kinky and unmanageable, assumed to be *"bad"* hair.

Where did that come from? It's all so shallow. Just like my nose I came to the conclusion my hair was good too. However, because of the belief that kinky hair equals bad hair I had to endure a hot pressing comb to straighten my hair.

My head and neck was often burned from not sitting perfectly still in the chair. I can remember ducking and dodging with anxiety every time mom removed the sizzling hot straightening comb from the stove.

I thought of plans to escape, if went to the bathroom I could bust out and run outside.

Mom was pleasingly plump and couldn't run as fast as me but I knew there would be a whooping when I came back. So I sat there and hollered, squirmed and cried. In addition my little sister's lips bloomed as she grew up, she was teased in school. She became self-conscience and sometimes tucked in her lips when she talked to people.

Because of all the stigma and controversy about facial features, body shapes, color and hair texture I began to wonder what's really going on.

As a young child I learned black people were made to believe and accept ourselves as inferior. We were deceived into this kind of thought process of who is better, more attractive and smarter. My mom didn't know she was raised to believe the same way.

Why is there a need to compare? we need to embrace differences and similarities of who we are and be at peace with it. I would never change my skin color under no circumstance; we come in shades of milk chocolate to dark cocoa brown.

We are like the color of rich dark coffee whose scent fills the air; laughing out loud while braiding our ebony hair. We blend in with God's rich brown earth soil. We walk proud in shades of cinnamon, mahogany, golden and even honey vanilla. As my sister grew older she accepted her looks and began wearing the reddest, brightest lipstick she could find.

I don't want to be no one's slave
Remembering Juneteenth 19th day in 1865

The big day had finally come January 1, 1863 when President Abraham Lincoln signed the Proclamation Declaration that all slaves should be freed. Now this freedom was proclaimed for only ten states since other states opposed Lincoln's order. Later on June 19th 1865. Two years after Lincoln's proclamation. General Gordon Granger declared Lincoln's plan to be executed that all slaves in the US be freed. There was an estimate of three million slaves in the US. Unfortunately, by this time Lincoln had passed away but his vision became a reality. When the news was announced to the slaves on the Evergreen Plantation in Edgard, Lousiana there was a scurrying around like you've never seen.

The slaves were overjoyed, confused and scared. Wilson and Bessie Mae Smith were busy packing up their meager belongings. They were in their late twenties now but were slaves since a child on this plantation. They had four year old twins, Wilson Jr and Florida Joy. Bessie Mae proudly put on her Sunday best hat the misses handed down to her while Wilson put on an old, but nice suit the master gave him. They smiled down at their twins glad they were being freed at a young age. They were heading up north to Wilson's uncle home who was one of the slaves freed by Harriet Tubman. When Wilson Sr. turned to glance one last time at the master's home and the cotton field he worked since he was ten years old he sighed, and said to Bessie Mae *"The massa can't pick cotton he ain't*

never done that before" Bessie thought and *said "The misses has never washed clothes in the boiling pot, cooked or even washed the dishes. She don't even know how to make clothes for her daughter, Susie Ann who is growing so big for her age"*
Wilson maybe we ought to go back and teach them how to do these things then leave in three months. Is that ok with you? he shook his head slowly saying yes ma'am.

They paused and proceeded to walk back to the plantation. Wilson Jr. who heard everything anxiously spoke up *"Mama, I don't like it when the Master puts his stinky, cold feet on my belly to warm them"* Then Florida Joy said *"I'm not a dog I don't want to walk on my knees no more while Susie Ann leads me around with her leash and tells me to bark"*

"No sir we don't want to go back"

You always said one day we was going to walk free let's go now they stomped their feet in unison.

When Florida Joy said that, they saw slaves walking along the road to freedom, smiling and running scared, looking back, sweating wiping their fore heads as if someone was running after them but no one was.

Wilson Sr. dropped his head for the first time he noticed the fresh brown dirt, he looked around and saw the flowers in full bloom for it was now July 1st ten days after June 19th he thought about the news from the grapevine from his uncle, Woodrow up North saying to come on up here we is waiting for you. He thought about last year's cold winter when he was out chopping wood for the master's fire place and accidently stepped on a rusty nail. His foot swelled up with a bad infection. He asked the master to see a doctor to tend to this infection but the master said *"Sorry Wilson I can't allow that I would get in big trouble this is not for your kind"* you might need to cut off the side of that foot that's infected. Wilson was discouraged with tears when he thought of all the years he's been a slave for this family. He also understood what the master was saying, those white folks doctor would refuse to help him. They would most likely chop his whole foot off and throw it in the garbage. Bessie Mae boiled some water added lye, corn whiskey and salt that burned like hell fire but healed his foot. Bessie Mae reflected on the time when she was going into early labor with the twins at six months the midwife cautioned her lay down for a few days to rest. She lost so much blood threatening to miscarriage the twins. After pleading with the master and misses to take a few days off her feet from picking cotton they gasped, turned their heads away from her and pointed her back to the cotton field.

Slowly she walked away she knew better to argue. She's done that before and was beat with a whip. The Lord blessed her to have those babies, healthy both at four pounds. The master didn't sell them like he did Bessie's baby brother, Leroy after he was weaned from her mama, Ms. Lucy Mae Charles may she rest in peace she wasn't the same after the massa sold Leroy.

She paused and thought of her mama and papa who passed away many years ago.

Soon out of Bessie's mouth before thinking she shouted, *"I want my twins to grow up free"* She covered her mouth hoping no one heard her. Wilson's eyes got big because he did hear her and responded *"You is right we have to go by hell or high water by the good Lord we is goin make it we ain't got no mo time to be no one's slave this place is not for us we must leave here"*

He smiled into the clear blue sky as the sun shone down on his face, he straightened his back, shifted his good foot forward and said Miss Bessie I want you to be able to sit down and rest when you want to as he grabbed her worn, calloused hands. I want our children to grow up with some dignity and go to college like those white children. I don't want my children to be slaves. I want to build us a home up north. Bessie cried *"Yes Sir I like that"* as she smiled, dried her eyes and positioned her hat. *Let's get going!*

The twins squealed with excitement *"hallelujah we is free"* All of a sudden they heard the misses scream through the kitchen window as she dropped a dish on the floor. *"Arthur I cannot do this kind of work"* they all looked at each other smiled, shrugged their shoulders and scurried down the dusty road singing glory, glory hallelujah since I laid my burdens down. I feel better so much better since I laid my burdens down. The twins skipping along holding hands had the biggest smile you ever seen.

Rise up from hating

"Can't we just all get along"

Pulled up by their own bootstraps yes that's what some will say, never stopping to think God gave them another day. Going around face in a scowl, looking to see who will stumble and fall.

Move yourself away from those who hate and despise for they are deceived and living a lie. Love is the answer whether you have riches or digging ditches.

"They'll say I can't stand her. Just look at that dress, she's tow up from the floor up; that hair is a hot mess! What makes people judge someone else? When they've never walked in their shoes, shared their misery or experienced their blues. No one knows the person behind the screen or the joys and heart-aches they've seen. God has a way of humbling folks and turning things around. That person may be rising up and the haters coming down. Let's reach out beyond ourselves and our needs and help someone else. Let love rise in our hearts, let's be the first to make that start. Search your hearts and let love be found.

Even the caterpillar couldn't keep his face to the ground. He emerged out of the cocoon rose up, looked around and flew the same thing can happen for me and you. There is someone that needs our smile to have strength to make that extra mile. You will be glad you made someone's day; shared their pain wiped their tears away.

Mighty Man of Valor
The chosen one

O' mighty man of valor do you know who you are?

You are God's chosen vessel from afar.

God has blessed you; the mantel he gives;

to seek and save the lost that they may live.

You were called from your mother's womb you are

fearfully and wonderfully made; to be a strong and

mighty soldier in Jesus Name.

So rise up and go, conquer and

claim the lost at any cost and bring praise to His name.

Don't put your hand to the plow or look back;

God is your shield remember,

He's got your back.

Seasons to rise
There is a time for everything under the sun

Seasons, dispensations of life, we are living in a world with much chaos, turmoil and strife. Blind hate has found a path into many lives. Skin color not the depth of one's heart or their mind causes people to judge our ways.
Deception layered with hate and lies; my prayer is that people will not only see but open their spiritual eyes. My beautiful mahogany black brothers and sisters I celebrate.
My sweet cornbread brown people I can relate. Only God knows your fate. I see the tears in your eyes concerned if your children will arrive home alive.

I share the pain in your soul the world can be mean, unloving and cold; let's embrace and remember our ancestors of times old. Who risked their lives, bled, fought, cried and died; that we would come forth to stand and rise.
Be encouraged my brothers and sisters and dry those weeping eyes put your hands on your hips but don't let your backbone slide. You must stand strong and tall but if the pain is too great and causes you to fall, and all you can do is muster up a crawl, crawl with dignity, crawl with pride.
Stand up on the inside and rise. Rise with determination. Rise above hate. Allow love to fill your heart with victory to celebrate.

Misunderstood Identity
Who do you think you are

A door mat sat on the porch becoming more and more frustrated that her only purpose appeared to be a designated place for anyone to walk all over her. She felt disregarded and disrespected for no one appeared to be grateful for her service. Back and forth people wiped their shoes on her. This abuse gave her lots of stress. She shivered from the cold air, wind and rain. She peeked in the home as someone slowly shut the door. She spotted a comfy chair sitting, warmed and sheltered from the cold, wind and rain.

She dreamed with anticipation of being a chair reserved for dignitaries. That's the life for me she thought, however, as she watched a bit longer the chair wobbled under the pressure of people of all sizes and shapes who plopped down in its lap.

Another day she seen people stick nasty chewing gum underneath the chair when no one was looking. How disrespectful she thought.

No, I'd rather not be a chair she decided and resolved to being a doormat.   A few months later summer came and the weather became warm.

The door mat heard the rustling of a ball rolling by. Kids down the street were happily playing catch. That's it she thought I will become a ball. No one can walk on or use me or wipe their dirty shoes on me I can move around and be fancy free.

39

The doormat believed herself into a ball and became content hoping now she would be happy and free. Soon she was tossed around from hand to hand, abused, shoved and kicked hard like a football.

She literally found herself short of breath and sore. Confused she decided to give up and resolve to her fate.

Later she was ignored and thrown in the backyard busted and bruised. She didn't have the strength to move around and be free. She wondered what was her purpose and destiny.

As she sat in the yard lopsided and sad she spotted dandelions sprawled out covering the ground. She admired their stamina, their toughness to remain stable allowing no one to uproot them...."*maybe that's what I should be*" Before she transformed herself into a dandelion a strong, calm yet strong voice from Heaven above said.
Do you know who you are? No said the ball.
The voice said, the time has come to reveal your true nature you have misunderstood your purpose and calling.

You are a black woman with ancestors who were captured, brainwashed and forced into slavery in country called America that is why you feel less than who you are. You never came to the full measure of your value. Sadly, internalized racism has been passed down many generations by your own people who were swayed from their worth as a human being.

However my child, you must rise up above this level of thinking and realize the roots of your ancestors and descendants from the mother land of Africa. You my dear like many others were birthed from Kings and Queens.

"I didn't know said the ball" I have been walked on, mistreated and disrespected all my life so I believed I was a nothing but a doormat"

I have been tossed around, beat down and kicked so hard I thought I was a ball. *"You are none of these"* the voice said from heaven.   However, the strong roots of the dandelion descend deep below the surface of the ground is the closet to your true nature. That is because no matter if the dandelion is uprooted, mowed down or yanked up with much force it has a spirit of tenacity on the inside that causes them rise. Black people have suffered many trials up to this time but no matter what has been done to Black people they have endured and always triumphed with power.

The dandelion when cut down is able to break and slip through concrete, soil and asphalt. Black people have that same spirit of resiliency. A people that has been continually beat down, lied on, abused, discriminated against, raped and murdered. Miraculously through my unseen power within the surface of your beings you have risen and still are here on this earth.

This attempt to keep black people down is counter-productive because in spite of it you have bounced back.

Black people are not standing in line waiting to jump off a bridge because of their financial hardships. You are survivors. You have been through the worst of times but I, your Lord have seen and carried you through it all.

Adversity has built strength, power and fortitude in your inner being. Sadly, this brainwashing has caused some of you to believe you are insignificant and of little worth.
It also creates a false sense of superiority in others. This is an illusion created in the minds of those who do not believe all men and women were created equal. It is not the color of anyone's skin for there is nothing inferior or superior in the melanin of anyone's skin tone.

I therefore charge you, Black man, black woman take your rightful place on this earth to be the shining stars you were created to be. Pass the baton to the next generation so they will know who they are. So they will never allow anyone to drag them down in believing they are inferior. Tell them not allow anyone to define their self-worth, authenticity or value.

From that day forward this black woman originally once a doormat began to stand tall and thrive in the light of her destiny walking proud and sharing her newly found self to others everywhere she went.

Justice Over-Ruled

**In memory of Michael Brown 18 yr old male gunned down
with up raised hands by the police in Ferguson, Missouri on
August 9, 2014
No charges were filed against the police, Darren Wilson**

Police officer your claim to fame is not wiping out our
black men; this kind of action is a no-win.

People of color everywhere represent this man
because this was a life you stole from God's hands.

People are praying for justice to rule; the plan to
eliminate black men is the Devil's tool.

The Bible says you will reap what sow; this fate
only God knows. You killed a son,
a friend and a brother.

Somewhere there is a fatherless child;
a weeping father and mother.

We are a people strong and we have endured long
many tragedies we have faced;

It's not your right to wipe out the black race?
You discharged your gun, his hands went up; he fell
down

All the people gathered around shocked and stunned
that you claimed justice by cowardly using your gun.

Read poems of God's love and deliverance.
You will find a few stories of how racism has impacted
lives and divided people.

Email: msgaile2002@yahoo.com
PO Box 5676
Kent, WA 98031
To order a copy go to: AMAZON.com
~~
*You will find this easy to read. You may laugh, cry and
just sit back and think.*
Linda Carter

~~
*Her poems are plain real, soulish and deep.
You must read them and become inspired*
Patricia Bruce

~~
*When I read the story about "Misunderstood Identity"
story I totally connected with the woman character.
At one time of my life it was me.*
Elizabeth Coleman
~~
Allow these poems and stories to do the healing you
need; Gail has an amazing gift.
Linda F.

Made in the USA
Columbia, SC
14 March 2020

89194919R00029